SHE
JUST
WANTS

To Virginia –
Woman to Woman –
Writer to Writer –

SHE *So Always,*

JUST

WANTS

by

Beverly Rollwagen

Beverly Rollwagen

NODIN PRESS

Cover image: Henri Matisse, *Rumanian Blouse*, 1936
courtesy The Baltimore Museum of Art
The Cone Collection, formed by Dr. Claribel Cone
and Miss Etta Cone of Baltimore, Maryland
BMA 1950.12.48 © 2004 Succession H. Matisse,
Paris / Artists Rights Society (ARS), New York

Acknowledgements

"Tea" and "Change" were first published in
Water~Stone, the Hamline Literary Review 2002.
I would like to express my gratitude to the McKnight
Foundation for a grant received in 2000, and to the
kind people at The Loft.

And for their support:

Thanks to Phebe Hanson. Thanks to Carol Connolly.
Thanks to Natalie Goldberg, Patricia Hampl, and
Michael Dennis Browne. Thanks to Pamela Holt,
JoAnn Verburg, Brigitte Frase, Jill Breckenridge, and
Sharon Chmielarz. Thanks to Jim Moore. Thanks to
Janet Kimmerle. Thanks to Norton Stillman at Nodin
Press. Thanks to Jonathon Lazear, Christi Cardenas,
and Wendy Lazear. Thanks to Jeff Shotts and John
Toren. Thank you to all who have shown kindness and
support, thank you.

And to John, Jake and Jenny, my love and gratitude,
always.

ISBN-1-932472-32-0
second printing

Nodin Press is a division of Micawber's, Inc.
530 N. Third Street, Suite 120
Minneapolis, MN 55401

For my mother and father,
Loraine and Clarence Baranowski

and for my JARs

CONTENTS

ONE 11-30

alone / art / babysitter / beauty
breasts / bus / change / child
cook / crush / dance / direction
down / dream / earthquake
employed / essential
exciting

TWO 31-52

famous / filled / forget / forever
gifts / grip / guess / guest / hat
help / honey / houses / incognito
incredible / intense / jealous / jezebel
kitchen / late / lazy
license

THREE 53-73

mailbox / marine / more / mouth
net / normal / o / ordinary
patient / perfect / phone / picture
play / queen / rain / reach
real

FOUR 75-94

secret / simplify / space / spinning
substitute / tea / test / time
under / understudy / verbs / waitress
warm /when / wrong / x-ray
yellow / yoga
zero

The great question that has never been answered, and which I have not yet been able to answer, despite my thirty years of research into the feminine soul is, "What does a woman want?"

Sigmund Freud

❦ ONE

alone

She just wants to be alone. To let her hair grow in peace. Others sweep at her with their tongues, and she agrees with them until they leave. They hold what she gives them in white gift boxes. They think they have her, but she parts with only light and air. She keeps everything of value deep within her, dark and safe.

art

She just wants to learn the art of forgiving. She looks in the phone book for a school, but no luck. She holds a grudge for so long that she cannot feel how heavy it is, how like a giant boulder between her shoulders. Like a Chinese gymnast, she learns to roll it back and forth, down to her fingertips, catching it just before it drops. The concentration keeps her going, alive with purpose. If she ever releases this ball of bitterness, she will float off into the sky. Nothing to hold her down, nothing of substance.

babysitter

She just wants to be a babysitter. To be picked up by the husband and ride in the front seat of a Buick, smelling his cologne, listening to his small talk. She wants to watch her neighborhood fall behind. After she feeds the kids, she lets them jump on the beds and play games so they'll like her. When the children are covered and asleep, she wants to look in their parents' room, to open their top drawer. She doesn't want to steal anything; she's not interested in their things, their secrets. She's looking for something specific. The cards. The birthday and anniversary cards. The wife usually keeps them, but sometimes it's the husband. They write of love and she can't imagine how it happened to these people. She holds the cards for a long time, knowing there must be a clue hidden within the script. A clue she can carry over into her own life, when it's time.

beauty

She just wants to give up the beauty part of this woman business. She feels not old and not young, which means she's old. She wants to tell the young woman to quit worrying about her appearance. "You are a great beauty," she whispers, "you remind me of myself at your age." As she moves away, she sees that her hands are her mother's hands, her neck her mother's neck. What is her mother doing without them?

breasts

She just wants to wear her breasts on the outside today. To give them an airing. She chooses the red basketball jersey, number 17, with white piping around the neck. She loops one loose armhole under each breast, and fastens the center with a rhinestone brooch. A pair of white shorts, very short, and black medium heels, because it is warm today and she will be walking. She checks the effect in her full-length mirror, for this is what women do. Front and back. Something is wrong; something is missing. She adds a black velvet hat, the one with the veil, and rhinestone earrings. Her breasts are relaxed and happy. She strolls through Paris, past the Deux Magots. Admiring murmurs from men. How easy fashion is, once you get the hang of it.

bus

She just wants to ride the bus today. She walks to the bus stop to stand with a stranger. The man steps off the curb to look into the distance as the bus rises over the hill. It looks like the bus will hit him, but it stops at his feet with a hiss. The driver hits the accelerator before they are seated and they swing from seat to seat like monkeys. Tree branches slap the side of the bus and push through the open window as they land in the same seat. They breathe a little faster, but do not allow their bodies to touch.

change

She just wants change. Not nickels and dimes. Big change. An ocean instead of a lake. The sun instead of a nightlight. She goes about her house and puts black where white used to be. She turns all the chairs upside down. When she realizes no one approves, she quietly puts everything back the way it was and goes to her room. There she gladly changes every cell in her body and presents herself again. She seems familiar to them; they don't guess why.

child

She just wants to be a child again. She remembers holding the hands of her parents, one on each side of her. There they go again, lifting her off her feet on the count of three. She never hears the count above her head, never sees it coming, the swinging of her body between them. This unbalancing act, this leaving the earth again and again for their pleasure. They tell her later that she begged for it.

cook

She just wants to cook for him. She won't do this every day; she wants to keep him on his toes. At first, she cooks every Monday, and the house fills with the smell of chicken in onions and peppers, crème caramel for dessert. Then days of nothing. He comes home to find her flipping through the pages of *Gourmet* and *Bon Appetit*, her cookbooks spread on the dining room table. She tells him she can't decide what to make; they'll have to go out. At the restaurant, she leans toward him to feed him a bite from her plate, something sharp and spicy, very different from what he ordered.

crush

She just wants to have a crush on him, private and harmless. Not like love, which requires so much. Crawling through the dark over ex-wives and lovers, picking out the shards of his truth. Try to love that. A crush is just feeling and fantasy, all buildup, no letdown. A rush toward accepting arms that aren't meant to hold her. No down payment and no forms to fill out. When she's finished, she doesn't even say good-bye; she just waves him off.

dance

She just wants to dance. A long time ago, she danced with boys. One summer night in the basement of a church, a boy led her to the center of the room. Slow dance, small town. He wasn't much taller than she, and their faces were very close. His shirt, washed and pressed by his mother, smelled clean. This made her trust him. They fit together and swayed, growing closer until he pressed his cheek to hers. Barely breathing. When it ended, they stepped apart, and she returned to her own body. He walked her home, silently, and she held his hand, stepping carefully over the cracks in the sidewalk, not wanting to fall with him.

direction

She just wants to know what direction she should take. She feels so lost. She follows a stranger home on the freeway. It is so comforting to trail after someone who knows where to turn, who even signals. There is an awkward moment when she pulls into his driveway and introduces herself to his family. They act like this has happened before. "Can you cook?" says the wife, narrowing her eyes.

down

She just wants to keep from going down for the third time. She sometimes forgets to breathe. She might be in danger of drowning, like her nose is just above the waterline. As a child, she jumped off the dock without fear, her body weight pulling her down through the cold. If only she could remember how far she had to go before she hit bottom. She is better at holding her breath underwater, where whatever brushes against her is supposed to be there.

dream

She just wants to dream. Everyone
tells her she does dream, but she
knows they lie to spare her feelings.
She plans each night carefully, inviting
dreams, even nightmares. A good falling
dream, where she wakes before striking
the ground, or a flying dream, swooping
under bridges, barely missing buildings.
Each night, she takes her hope to bed,
and her longing fills the room. When
morning comes she runs water over
her wrists, waiting for it to grow hot.
Watching how it circles a little, like
everything else, before it disappears.

earthquake

She just wants the earth to move for her. She once heard the love cries of a Japanese woman through the walls of the Okura Hotel in Tokyo. Later the same night, an earthquake swayed the building, and she woke to watch the lampshade tremble across the room. She thought of the Japanese couple rocking together, the earth shifting and sighing under them, the man's eyes closed, the woman's open.

employed

She just wants to be employed for eight hours a day. She is not interested in a career; she wants a job with a paycheck and free parking. She does not want to carry a briefcase filled with important papers to read after dinner; she does not want to return phone calls. When she gets home, she wants to kick off her shoes and waltz around her kitchen singing, "I am a piece of work."

essential

She just wants to keep her essential sorrow. Everyone wants her to be happy all the time, but she doesn't want that for them. There is value in the thread of sadness in each person. The sobbing child on an airplane, the unhappy woman waiting by the phone, a man staring out the window past his wife. A violin plays through all of them, one long note held at the beginning and the end.

exciting

She just wants everyone to know how exciting life is today. Even the trees bleat with pleasure. People are too busy to notice, so she does a little dance for them. They make little circles in the air until she stops. For her to be quiet is all they want; for them to fly is all she wants. The day leaks away as the sun shines beyond understanding.

❧ TWO

famous

She just wants to be famous. To run from photographers, to duck into limousines with a handsome man holding her hand. She would lift the beaded hem of her dress to expose her slippered foot. This is a fairy tale. She is too plain to be a movie star, too short to be a supermodel, too lazy to shop for a beaded dress and slippers. A handsome man would grow annoying, and photographers are a nuisance. Really, she just wants to be lost in the crowd, watching.

filled

She just wants to be filled. Sated. She walks from room to room wearing her hunger like a heavy scent. It's good to know the same need as everyone else, but hers is a large empty field in winter. She opens cupboards crammed with food and shuts them again. It's not food she wants. It's nothing to do with the mouth and tongue. It's a great howling within that she's afraid to let out, knowing that it will consume her.

forget

She just wants to make him forget the women in his past. Especially his first love, the one who formed his opinion of women. She finds old photographs of them, hand in hand, smiling. She watches his eyes when he speaks of her, and asks questions about what they did together, where they went on dates, what drew him to her. He believes she is truly interested in his life and doesn't hesitate to answer. He never feels the edge of the razor as she carefully excises the image of the other woman, but he feels a small stirring as she slips into place beside him. She takes his hand, and they smile for the camera.

forever

She just wants to last forever. She's afraid to be in the sun because of cancer, afraid to eat red meat, to drink martinis, ride with strangers, watch television, read in dim light, shake hands, kiss the dog, handle money, spray the rosebushes, wear makeup, walk in the rain. She sits near her front window day after day, behind the curtain, watching her hands drift in her lap. This is the way to age gracefully, she thinks. Forgetting about the birds and their singing.

gifts

She just wants to stop all the complaining. Her own and others. When her son says he hates having flat feet, she reminds him of boys with no feet. He rolls his eyes. "Your eyes work," she says. "Your eyes and your mouth and your brain." Your flat feet will keep you out of the army, a place of guns and blood and death. God bless your flat feet, she thinks. God bless all your gifts.

grip

She just wants to get a grip. She slips a little more each day. Today she lost her glasses and forgot to remember something important, but she couldn't think of what it was. It's difficult clinging to an image she's held so long: of a capable and sensible woman. Not this dreamy sap. She opens the refrigerator to make something for dinner, but the shelves are bare. She remembers she was supposed to go grocery shopping yesterday. She swings the refrigerator door back and forth, fanning herself with cool air. It reminds her of winter, and ice-skating, skimming over the frozen water on quick, silver blades. She was always good at going backwards.

guess

She just wants to guess what he wants. At first, she thought: children. But that wasn't it. She wants to be methodical, not reckless, so she makes a list of everything she knows he likes. And another list of everything he doesn't. Sometimes there is crossover. He likes to talk but not as much as she. He even puts his hands over his ears because he can't listen anymore. Then she can't stop talking, and her voice circles the room with no place to land, a bird trapped in a room full of windows. Years later, she will find the door and fly out.

guest

She just wants to be a guest, a
houseguest. She wants to arrive
at the front door, be led into a formal
room and invited to sit, to rest before
going further. Tea and a dainty cake
with pink icing placed before her. Then
the trip upstairs to her room, her bag
unpacked, her dress pressed and hung on
a padded hanger, her nightgown sprayed
with lavender and arranged on the bed.
At dinner, she entertains her hosts with
stories and gentle jokes. They escort her
to her room, but stop short of actually
tucking her in. She stays the weekend,
and sends a charming note within two
days, written at an antique French desk
in yet another guest room. This one
with a bay window, overlooking a private
garden. She notices roses clinging to the
trellis, and thinks: how obvious.

hat

She just wants to wear a hat. Not a girlie hat with flowers, a hard hat with her name on it, like a steelworker. She walks along the edge of the girder as if it were as wide as a sidewalk, guiding the next beam into place. She stands with her arms crossed over her orange vest, looking down through clouds and rain. At the end of the day, she whistles all the way home in her pickup. On the days she feels edgy, she stays on the job after everyone else leaves. Then she sits on the top girder, lets her legs drift in space, and listens to what can't be seen.

help

She just wants to help. She reads the paper every morning and writes the names and places of all the people she might be able to assist. This takes hours. Then she gets her checkbook and begins to write checks to the most needy. When her checks are gone, she sends the cash from her wallet. When her cash is gone, she sells her house, her car, her furniture, her jewelry. She sends the proceeds to deserving people and begins to feel good about herself. Her self-esteem is definitely up. When she is down to the clothes on her back, she keeps just enough to buy a Sunday paper and opens it to Help Wanted.

honey

She just wants honey. Sweeter than sugar, and with as many flavors as flowers, depending on where the bees land. She's been called "honey" a few times: a lover, her mother, strangers who don't know her name but think they recognize something sweet about her. As a child she licked the inside of her wrist to find out if she had a taste. Salt and dirt and weeds. Sweet wasn't in there anywhere.

houses

She just wants new houses one after
another until she owns an entire city
block. Or, her own suburb with a blue
gas station. It is so easy to make everyone
angry, to watch them cry. This bit of
knowledge makes her careful. She listens
to individual sounds and doesn't eat for
days. Then she eats the table and the
couch. When he comes home, he says
nothing. He notices all the bare space
and smiles. She loves making him so
happy.

incognito

She just wants the city to stop changing. One day a park, the next day a parking lot, as if it's trying to go incognito. She wonders where the birds and squirrels live. A Buick pulls out of the new lot and pauses as the automatic guard arm lifts for it to pass. As it pulls in front of her, she sees the bright eyes of an animal in the back window, next to the box of Kleenex and the umbrella. He salutes with his bushy tail. The man driving the car has a nose like a beak.

incredible

She just wants him to think she's incredible. But she hasn't met him yet so she decides to practice conversations in her head. Oh, but she's witty and bright when she's alone! He is her dream lover and does everything right without being asked. She rehearses every minute of every hour she will spend with him. It's why her friends say she has such a hard time finding a real man. She gets bored before their first date and she's just ending their last fight as he rings her doorbell, holding those silly, hopeful flowers.

intense

She just wants to paint the world
a different color. It's too intense,
too bright. She admires a lot of dead
painters, the ones who blurred bridge
and sky, water and woman. She's told
to squint into the light to allow colors
to swim together, so she leans out her
open window, presses her hands over her
eyelids, and lets a crack of light seep in
along the seam of lashes. She likes the
world this way; she likes not really being
able to see.

jealous

She just wants to put her head in his lap. But she doesn't know him well enough, although she has been his dinner partner for nearly four hours. She laughed at all his jokes, listened and nodded at everything he said, and now she's tired. There is a price to pay for being polite, for being good. If she could rest her head in his lap for five minutes and have him pass his heavy hands across her brow, she knows she would feel better. She feels like the flowers painted along the edge of the china dishes, beautiful and delicate but flattened for good. She is so jealous of them as the server lifts her plate carefully and carries it away.

jezebel

She just wants to be sultry, like Joan
Crawford as Jezebel. Or was it Bette
Davis. She wants to look directly at
the camera, no faking, nothing coy. A
dangerous woman. She wants to smoke
and drink and wisecrack like a man, to
arrange her hair over her shoulders, one
curl pulled forward, as calculated as her
evening ahead. Will she let him slide
the black lingerie down her body? Will
it pool on the floor between them? Or
will she light a cigarette and blow smoke
into his eyes as she laughs in his face?

kitchen

She just wants to scrub the kitchen floor, but a woman in her position isn't supposed to get her hands in hot water. She waits until they're all asleep before she sneaks downstairs. Her knees groan as she shifts her weight on them, back and forth across the floor. This mindless dance eases her so much, she hums. The floor shines in the moonlight as she walks slowly upstairs. In bed, he turns toward her and takes her hands, hot and raw. He loves the smell of her fingers, their strange taste.

late

She just wants to be on time. She's been late so often, distressing people she loves. She decides to arrive ten minutes early for every occasion. This means, when invited for dinner she must sit outside in her car. It's so rude to catch the host and hostess in their underwear, or in a domestic dispute over the division of duties. She plans carefully to be the first to arrive, to catch them in that breathless, excited state, ready for anything. For a few moments, she has their total attention.

lazy

She just wants to let the lazy water fall around her. Someone calls it rain, but that comes with sky-splitting speed. What she wants now is the calming steadiness of a shower. The water should not be cold. She should feel every pore of her body being filled. She will tip her head back, open her mouth and receive what the sky gives. This is a perfect way to drown.

❧ THREE

license

She just wants to renew her driver's license. In her wallet, a woman with a funny haircut looks out of a clear plastic window. This can't be me, she thinks. If she's going to lie about her age and weight, she might as well be more creative. She hires a model for the photo, a woman who doesn't look so startled in bright light. A woman who really looks good in leather.

mailbox

She just wants to slip into the mailbox on the corner. She makes herself very small and eases into the slot. She times it perfectly: the box is half full and the next scheduled pickup is two hours away. This gives her enough time to sort the mail into two piles: Interesting and Not Interesting. Interesting consists of personal letters. Everything else is Not Interesting. She throws Not Interesting in one corner and sits on them while she reads. One letter opens: "Dear One, I have met someone new but hope we can always be friends." One lovely lie after another slides down the page in looping script. She folds the letter carefully before putting it back in its envelope. A good letter should have a beginning, a middle and an end, she thinks, not just an end.

marine

She just wants to storm his beach. She wouldn't mind a little training: a ropes course, a three-hour morning run, a good physical. He seems dug into his position and he's holding firm, but he's never gone hand to hand with her, and she wants to be ready. She dons her camouflage and face paint; she cleans her weapon. He's well within range now, but she's patient; she waits for darkness. She wants the element of surprise, the pounding waves, the danger as their currents come together, circling and mingling.

more

She just wants more than five minutes.
She knows that how you do anything
is how you do everything. She slows
down to pay attention to the red line
of the cardinal, the pulse in her lover's
throat, a shadow across her child's face.
This leaves only five minutes to live the
rest of her life, to get where she's going.
Hurry slowly, she reminds herself, hurry
slowly.

mouth

She just wants to follow her father's advice: "Keep your eyes and your ears open and your mouth shut." Such good advice, but so late to start. She begins after his death, after she asks the mortician about her father's mouth as he lies in his casket. He tells her he sews the mouth closed from the inside, to keep it from falling open. All during the funeral, she weeps for the loss of his voice in the world. Later, she learns to grieve with her eyes open, knowing he is somewhere, watching and listening, wanting to speak.

net

She just wants a net under her like the one she saw at the circus. Bodies fell out of the air, white and silent, caught on the breath of children. She wants to know the thrill of falling from a great height, feeling sure she will be suspended and held. Her life is a series of risks, and she wants to stand on the edge, catch the bar, and swing out over the crowd as the clowns hold the net taut and ready.

normal

She just wants to be normal. To sleep at night and stay awake during the day. But her days and nights fight like siblings that she can't separate. When she had babies, she held them at night, grateful for their company. It gave her time to listen to them before they learned to speak. Now the night invites her to sit in the rocking chair and sing the lullaby her babies loved. Sending her to a place as distant and bright as the moon, as far away as a dream.

o

She just wants to live in peace. She
wants this for everyone. She is
deeply disturbed by the news of war, but
no matter how much money she sends
or how much she prays, a garden of guns
blooms somewhere in the world. Over
and over again, she sees the same picture
on the front page: the child sprawled
dead in the street, the mother looking
into the camera, her mouth forming a
perfect o. Even from this far away, she
can hear the sound it makes. It follows
her from room to room.

ordinary

She just wants to call in sick. She's not sick, but she feels something coming on that alters her ability to perform the ordinary, the expected. She places the back of her hand against her forehead, as her mother did. After making the call to her boss, she feels quite well, quite like herself again. She spends the day singing; she speaks to no one, nearly delirious with joy. The next day she tells them, "Fever. I had a strange fever all day."

patient

She just wants to be more patient. She knows that patience is a sign of maturity, but today she feels five years old. Waiting in line at the airport, she begins to tap her foot. By God, she does have rhythm. She changes her ticket and flies to New York to study all forms of dance before she settles on flamenco. She loves to toss her head with disdain, to kick her ruffled skirt about. In Spain, that passionate place, she spins and stamps her feet at her lover. He doesn't call her childish. He calls her an artist and showers her with gifts.

perfect

She just wants everything to be perfect. Her children were perfect when she first got them, but now they're getting wrecked like the furniture. She lies in bed all night rearranging them and all she gets is tired and sidelong looks from him. He knows he's next and steps out of her path at every opportunity. She will get him though. She will make his life perfect.

phone

She just wants everyone to get off the phone. They act like they're so important. Everywhere she goes she hears ringing, and tinny little songs coming from purses and pockets. Snippets of classical music played at the wrong speed. She decides to act like a VIP too; she buys a tiny phone and holds it to the side of her head like a seashell. "Hello? Hello?" She hears the roar of the ocean, with its tidings from beyond.

picture

She just wants to stop seeing the picture of the young woman in the newspaper. The one who hanged herself. She'd been raped, her parents killed, and now no man would marry her. She sees how the girl's neck tilts slightly as if she's listening to music and how her hair curls over her forehead as if to protect her privacy. It is early morning, the mist rising in the far-off field. The branch does not bend from the weight of her body; its leaves do not cover her. As if she belongs there, as if she's a natural part of the tree. Soon, the men will cut her down. She will fall into someone's arms, and he will hold her for a moment. He will hold her and it will look something like love.

play

She just wants to play like a child again. There are so many games, and she's forgotten the rules. She recalls winning a few times, the short stack of paper money in her fist. She remembers games of running and falling and the way speed made her feel like she could fly. She understands people who lean over bridge railings too far, who fall toward the water. Those who couldn't say what they wanted, who didn't leave notes.

queen

She just wants to wait at the curb forever. She doesn't care if the cab comes or not. Songs play in her head from the night before; the stars still hang in the sky. And a pale moon. This is when she realizes the difference between alone and lonely: alone with the sky and the sharp air, lonely in the backseat of a taxi, rushing into the world. She waves like a sad queen as they pull away from the curb.

rain

She just wants the rain to stop. But she is not in charge of rain, just as she is not in charge of memory. That small, steady beat in her. The first time she had a massage, she cried when her spine was touched, and she saw her dead father alive again, laughing. The masseuse told her that memories are stored in different parts of the body, and went on stroking her. Now, she sees so many people every day, holding themselves carefully, trying not to touch or be touched.

reach

She just wants to reach out and stroke his back. In the middle of the night. But she doesn't, and he sighs and moves away. Her inaction is the beginning of regret. To be one with him is what she wants, but he is so far from her, she barely recognizes him. She opens her mouth to whisper his name, but nothing comes out.

real

She just wants the flowers in the vase to be real. They are too perfect, petals pointed and unscarred, none missing. She knows that real flowers are flawed and bruised, quivering with a torn delicacy. Especially at the center, where the bees beat their wings.

secret

She just wants to know your secret. She won't tell if you've had an affair, or your face lifted, or when you last made love. She won't tell if you're pilfering from the office, or gambling when you're supposed to be at the hospital visiting your mother, or what you would do for money. Strangers tell her the most unlikely things, and she never repeats them. Once, a woman told her she carried a gun. Silver with a mother-of-pearl inlay on the handle, a little jewel. She opened her purse, and the gun rested in its own velvet pocket, ready and dangerous. Like every secret.

FOUR

simplify

She just wants to simplify. To be owned by less. She buys a smaller house, one-half the size of the first one. She gives half of everything away. She does this again and again until she can live in her car. She divides the day into simple tasks: eating, working, playing. At night she sits on the hood of her car, watching the sky fill with stars. It's the only time she feels reckless and rich; she never has to give one star away.

space

She just wants space. An area of emptiness surrounding her, devoid of sound, of smell. Comprised of air. She decides to separate from him and slowly disengages her arms and legs. Untangling her hair from his takes much longer. She must lift one strand at a time to keep from hurting him. Gradually, she feels them dividing, much as cells divide, two from one. Not like Siamese twins, who lose so much when cut apart. Free now to take a step back, she sees where the knots that held them together have cut into them. The scars are raised and can be read like braille.

for Carol Connolly

spinning

She just wants to stop spinning her wheels. It seems like she was in this exact spot last year, and the year before. Time is so elusive and can't be held in both hands. She sits watching the sun go up and come down each day, marveling at its consistent effort, forgetting to count the minutes. She can't remember if someone told her how long she'd be on earth, or what she should do. They only said that the earth is spinning too.

substitute

She just wants to find a substitute for love. In cooking, certain ingredients can be used in place of others: applesauce for oil, or carob for chocolate. But the refined palate can always taste the difference, and she has a refined palate for love. Even though she knows there is nothing like the real thing, she takes little bites of what passes before her, just to keep her appetite under control.

tea

She just wants tea in the afternoon. Not with a ceremony. Not with deferential women serving, bowing. More like the Savoy Hotel, three o'clock and a harpist in a black gown, the low-cut back revealing her muscles, as she rocks forward to pluck the long, vibrating strings. She sits behind the music, on a plush love seat as a pale waiter in a tuxedo serves the tea. Without looking at her, with no interest in her. He cares only for the proper placement of the silver, the china cup and saucer, the timing of the delicate food. She begins to care about sugar and hot milk, berry jam and clotted cream. How thin the cucumber, how thick the butter. She need never be hungry again. The deer gather against the walls and make no sound.

test

She just wants to be more selective.
Her friends seem to choose her; she
goes with the first caller. This explains
all her old boyfriends, too. It takes time
to be choosy, to hold to high standards.
Like a university admissions department,
she decides to give a test, to require
an essay explaining exactly why she
should accept you. Space is limited. She
prepares a reception for all applicants and
she looks forward to meeting you. Don't
bring any luggage yet.

time

She just wants to locate herself in time and space. Everything rushes past: childhood, beauty, even pain. There must be a place to rest, to take a deep breath and absorb what's gone before. She watches the face of the clock for a clue; she studies the map of her life. She notices how she's been all over, and never too long in one place. She can't decide if this is a problem or a gift. She points to a dot on the map and decides to settle there. She wants to believe that there is still time for a mailbox with her name and address in block letters. Still time to go home.

under

She just wants to live under the bed.
Voices call to her, but she lets them
float to the next room and then the next.
In a short time, she is nocturnal and is
able to stalk through the night, peering
around the legs of chairs, hiding behind
draperies. She slides back under the bed
before morning, just in time to watch
the man swing his legs to the floor near
her face. He yawns. He has no idea how
thin his ankles look. She almost comes
out.

understudy

She just wants an understudy, a body double for the days when she does not feel like appearing in any of the roles she has assumed and/or been assigned. She places an ad in the paper. Wanted: one wife, mother, daughter, neighbor, friend. Live-in OK. Own car necessary. No lines to memorize; everything ad-libbed. No days off.

verbs

She just wants to live in France. Not forever. Just long enough to separate the nouns from the verbs, the masculine from the feminine. She is trapped inside the cage of her own language, with very few clues from the natives. One day they won't speak to her at all, the next she is treated with kindness and offered food and wine. She believes it has something to do with the bridges of Paris. The constant crossing over water, and the many monuments. One night an artist named Christo wrapped the Pont Neuf in canvas. She walked across with a crowd of people, all of them startled out of language, all of them listening to the sound of their muffled footsteps, foreign and faintly musical.

waitress

She just wants to be a waitress. To learn the exquisite timing necessary to appear at your elbow while you're still undecided, and then vanish until you've grown moss on your north side. She wants to tell you all about herself and then forget to place your order with the cook. When you're wild with hunger, she wants to place the plate with the wrong food before you. She knows how to dip her head with sorrow at the way things go wrong in the world. From her, you learn your place. She watches you leave your money near the plate, and she accepts the small kiss you leave on your napkin.

warm

She just wants to be warm. She thought passion would do it, but she almost died from the burning it brought. She decides to place thermostats on each floor reading seventy-two degrees, summer and winter. No more flaming out because of love, no more living below zero. She buys a down jacket and puts her hands into her pockets as she steps outside. She feels how the geese desire to lift off, to fly away to the heat. She's afraid to follow her instinct. She walks with her head lowered, grounded and solitary, as mothers and children flock to the playground.

when

She just wants a refill. She holds out her cup and the waiter pours hot coffee into it, but she wants more. She has heard that too much of everything is just enough, and that's all she wants. He wants to please her, so he lets the coffee spill over the rim of the cup, onto the saucer, onto the table, the floor, and finally it runs like a river out the door. She smiles at him. "When," she says.

wrong

She just wants him back when she gets lonely. She remembers how he smiled at her when they first met. Maybe he wasn't so bad. She picks up the phone and presses the first three digits of his number. Her friends never liked him, but he treated her well enough around strangers. In private, though, he looked past her or through her; she felt invisible. She puts the phone down. She remembers how he yawned when she told him she loved him, how he said she was so transparent. She lifts her face to look in the mirror, and she is not made of glass, but is both solid and abundant. Wrong, she thinks. He is still wrong.

x-ray

She just wants to dissect their marriage. At the very least, get an x-ray. She wants to see what holds it all together, without being too invasive. She's watched many healthy unions break apart from one fall, and she wants to be sure the bones she's counting on are strong enough to keep them erect. There are shadows between them already, she sees, as she holds their film up to the light.

yellow

She just wants to drive a yellow car. Any size, any shape. She's heard that yellow cars get involved in the fewest accidents. Lately, she feels vulnerable, hurtling along the freeway, other cars passing her on the left and the right, the car behind her nudging her along, right up to the posted speed. She doesn't have the courage to whip into the passing lane; she doesn't know any evasive tactics, and she doesn't want to test the limits. She thinks that all these drivers must have driven cautiously when they took the test to get a driver's license. Where is the Examiner now?

yoga

She just wants to be more flexible.
She takes a yoga class and begins to
feel her breath move through her; she
learns to send it down to her bones. It
is shy at first, tentative. A small wind
rustling at the back of her throat.
In time, her breathing grows strong
and reliable, and she can bend in any
direction without breaking. She feels
the mind follow the breath like a trusting
child. The kind of child who observes
everything, who holds pain without
dropping it, without crying out.

zero

She just wants to feel light. She begins with her hair and cuts it so short her ears look like the Buddha's, with lobes as long as tongues. She looks ridiculous, but without the distraction of hair, she has a lot more time to think. She eliminates makeup, then stockings and heels, and stops eating food she has to cook. She wears the loose, comfortable robe of a priest. Her life looks different now. She spends more and more time alone; she finds her old friends to be a heavy load, asking questions she can't answer like, "What are you doing?" when she is busy being. Inside she carries a great nothingness, a zero, the zero at the beginning.

Beverly Rollwagen lives with her husband and two children in Minneapolis, Minnesota. She writes poetry and prose and received a McKnight Fellowship in Creative Prose. She has been nominated for a Pushcart Prize and is currently working on her second book.